LUSCIOUS BANE

Hikari Syuu

The characters and events portrayed in this book are fictitious. Any similarity to real persons, living or dead, is coincidental and not intended by the author.

ASIN : B0B7L1KM8W
ISBN : 9786299712909

Cover design by: Hikari Syuu
Published by Nursyuhada Zulkifli
Lot 16005, Jalan Maarof, Kampung Rimba Terjun, 82000 Pontian, Johor.

To my beloved parent and cats whom always cherish me throughout my life with an endless beam of love and support. I love you to the moon and back.

CONTENTS

LETTERS FOR READER

Dear readers,

All characters in this short story are merely work of fiction for entertainment purposes. Also, I would like to warn that there might be mild content of harsh languages as this story was based on real life experiences by a local student in Malaysia. The theme contained in this book would be a toxic friendship between two people whom has been treating like sisters for years. I apologize for any discomfort in this book that you may find it sensitive. Overall, the flow of this story are meant as learning lesson that we all can take by the end of this story. Thank you, and wish you have a good time reading.

Love,
Hikari Syuu

LUSCIOUS BANE

Bane.

A noun that stands for poison. Destruction and death. Slayer. Killer. Also for curse, and woe. In chiefly Scotland, it is referred to as bane.
Luscious.

Well, it means pretty. Something pleasant to look at. Harmless, even. No one would have expected a beautiful thing could be so venomous.

Right?

I'm afraid those ideas are rather far-fetched.

Maybe it's true pretty things are harmless. An innocent being as well. Correct? Well, I would have the same thought as you in this case.

But not when you've truly discovered their true nature...personally. By that time, you've probably had a second thought. It could be the last chance to save yourselves.

Or.

You could never be able to run away from it.

Like I did.

♦♦♦♦♦♦

They say that friendships are beautiful. Even My Little Pony once said that friendship is magic. My poor naïveté soul once held into those possibilities. Think that every human being is meant for a decent bond called friendship. A genuine bond requires sacrifice, they say. And my dear thoughts constantly purposely blinded what I've seen and learned about my friendship with her —believing that not everything I've seen is what I was thinking. It could have been a misunderstanding, I thought. People possess various qualities of behaviors after all. Or maybe, I'm the only one that is an oddball amongst normal people. Either way, this was how my perspectives on friendship changed over the years. I do hate to admit that my opinion differs from others, but that's just what my experience made me think so. Neither would I blame them for it. I'll just consider it as some sort of Fate.

I wasn't sure how exactly how our friendship bloomed, but all I did remember was that our first meeting sparked on the first day of orientation at a local university in Machang. Applied for Diploma in Administrative Science. Not exactly what I had in mind, but, I'll just go with the flow since my qualification for English Literature Programme isn't above par. It's fine. Rather than being an aimless wanderer, I'll just enter any program that fit my current qualifications. Learning something new is fine by me. I wouldn't mind learning things that I never thought of. How worse can it be? Well, except for math I think. Man, I always find it like a love-hate relationship with that subject. I don't hate it, yet I find it intriguing as well, but I hardly fall in love with it because my understanding of those numbering principles isn't exactly parallel to what should be expected. And yet, I did what I can. Okay, let's get back to the story.

Our friendship started when I helped her carry some of her heavy bags to the assigned dorm. It's just an act of humanity, that's all. I didn't expect to befriend anyone on my first day.

Turned out we became close after that. The room had two double-decker beds. Means we get to have another two new friends in a room beside me and her. "Hey, ummm...Can I sleep on the lower bunk? I'm not used to the height." She softly chuckles. That's my very first time hearing such rationale but I'm okay with it. Everyone is different. "Sure," I said. She started to introduce herself to me. "I'm Dhia, by the way." She smiled sweetly. "I'm Fida." I don't know if I smiled back at her but I think I did.

Machang was one big rural area in Kelantan from my observation as we discovered the area together. Well, four of us. It was fun. The other two used to throw sarcastic jokes at times. I'm not sure about Dhia, but I find it rather quite uncomfortable. I felt like it can be too far when one of them kicked a stray cat away for begging for food. Dhia told me that it was normal and even told me to become open-minded about it. I simply just sigh and nod to her statement. Not that I purely agree with that term. It's just that I find it rather overboard to shoo those creatures away in a rude manner. For god's sake, animal food can be five times more expensive than human food. I knew that because I had cats and the experiences of taking care of them. Even the flavors are close to T20's exclusive dining despite being an animal's food. Fresh shrimp with Mackerel, Ocean Tuna, Scallop, and also veggies for a balanced diet. Just name it. "Sorry...I'm used to having cats as my best friend." I honestly didn't know why I spill the truth to her. My heart told me that she can be trustworthy. Didn't seems like she was choosing a side. "It's okay...Just be cool with it next time. Okay?" This said. I accepted her advice with an open heart. Guess there's a lot more to learn from that day onwards.

Making friends wasn't as breezy as it looks on TV or from random aunties' stories when they're sharing about their youth. I did feel quite an envy. How I wish my friendship journey would be as beautiful as theirs as well. I find it struggles to get used to them. Finding the middle ground without being insensitive can be tricky. Sometimes I am quite confused on what are the things that are sensitive to be said to them and which ones aren't. Trying my best to be open-minded while fitting in with their stupid jokes by becoming one turned out weren't exactly helping me to befriend people. Throwing jokes similar to them only made me earned an awkward silence from them. As if indicating that they find it offensive. I admit I find it excruciating to be a hypocrite with myself. Silly me. I disregard such thoughts instead. Thinking I've been narrow-headed while foolishly forcing myself to meet people's expectations when it comes to socializing.

I told my mum about it, inquiring about her opinion. She said not to mind much about those matters and just focus on studying. Again, nodded to it open-heartedly. And so I focused on studying. Making friends is a second thing. No rush. "Study is important, but so does social. You can't just waltz into life without learning how to make friends with people. It's an important skill in the real world." Dhia constantly advised me on socializing. She even gave me tips on socializing with people. Mean, lame jokes are also part of the normal thing, she said. Speaking of lame, mean jokes, Dhia, too, eventually became the duo's victim. The two occasionally spatted her for playing two sides. Silly dear me, I felt sympathy for her. Upon sharing similar predicaments, the two of us became close. Like sisters. Dhia and I soon spent time as besties. We went to the canteen and classes together. Judging how she got the hype over socializing with people and seems much more energetic, also the way she insisted me to be more open and social like her, I had a feeling she's an extrovert.

"Come on, let's dance together!" She pulled me to join her.

I crinkled my nose as I politely refuse her idea, "Nah, I'm good."

"Alaa...you're just being shy lah..." She assumed me as a shy person. I kept it silent and simply smile.

"I need to study..." I said.

“We can study anytime, Fida.” She suggested. “You and I can study together. Don’t worry! Now come on!” Dhia giggled while coaxing me to join her by pulling my arm. By the time the duo, Suria, and Rose, went home during the weekend, the two of us enjoying ourselves with the upbeat music. Softly sighed, I close my textbook and join her. Only like few minutes after that before I let her enjoy her time dancing to the music. I’m not sure why but I find it exhausting, so I continue revising the Accounting subject after joining her for some time. I didn’t hate it. Just felt myself growing tired with the dancing, that’s all.

Lunch was usually the similar thing we had on previous days. Even on weekends. Oh, the funny thing about a weekend in the Kelantan area. Unlike Selangor and Kuala Lumpur, the weekend here was Friday and Saturday. North region like Kelantan, Terengganu, and Johor had their weekend on Friday and Saturday. Quite shocking at first because most students from the region like Selangor and KL had a weekend on Saturday and Sunday. Mom and Dad quite worried at first if I were to live out-of-town places. Getting to know the places, I assured them that scrumptious delicacies are sold everywhere in Machang. Commonly we had Nasi Kukus for lunch if we ever walked down from the UTM gate. Sometimes *Tom Yam, Nasi Kerabu* or *Nasi Dagang* on the other days. Hanging out with two other classmates —Hanna and Tijah. They’re a bunch of nice people. A bit different from Rose and Suria. Of course, they too, occasionally throw silly jokes, but not as snarky as those two. These two seem to be more friendly. The four of us – Hanna, Tijah, Dhia, and me, went to the library together after lunch sometimes. Mostly Dhia was the one who proposed to teach us the subjects. She’s an excellent student and explained it very well. She gave me chance to teach the three of them, but the message probably sounds misleading from what I hope to share with them based on my understanding. Hence, she politely took over the matter and re-explain to all of us more simply.

Studying here in Machang was okay, I guess. There's nothing wrong with the lectures. The lecturers were pretty much helpful in assisting the students. I just need to do a lot of past year questions to tackle the given problem yet it felt never enough. Dhia always came up to have every one of us study together. Usually, when the exam was getting near, we were all grouped to cram the subject. It was fun, although at times I felt that my mind was technically suffocated over the matter of getting fit into normal people's common norms. Small things like using a pencil while doing past year questions. Rose and Suria noticed my behavior and straightly question my preferences in using pencil over pen while revising, saying that university students should be using pens all the time, and pencils are just for high school kids. I tried to ignore their advice this time by simply humming to the matter but Rose, Suria, including Dhia herself, urged me to change it to pen instead. For god sake, it's just a mechanical item to write. Do these people accept my rationale on that small matter? Sadly no because that's not how university students should be. "You'll thank us later knowing this fact, Fida...You won't regret this. Trust me." Dhia said. I'm not that stupid, you know. I can change the mechanical usage when the time needs it. Feeling lazy to argue further, I simply thanked them and press onward with my revision. The only thing I tried to avoid but find it is when it comes to socializing. Not everyone was mean in my class. There were a few good guys who seem friendly as well. And chirped along responding to him via Whatsapp.

"Ohayogozaimasu!" He said. No one seem to answer him, though.

"Ohayo, Rosman!!" I replied him on the group. Just been a casual friend, nothing more. Really thought people were unbothered to those things, until one girl from certain group interrupted the friendly conversation in the group chat.

"I didn't know anything about Ohayo but I sure know Go To Die!" She replied as soon as I replied to Rosman.

The chat eventually stopped right away. Not sure if she had different sense of humour, purposely tried to put a stop to the Romanized Japanese conversation, or simply been straight out rude.

Dhia was fully aware that I'd been bullied by Rose and Suria. I think that's probably the reason why she sort of encouraged me to keep pushing forward to have good marks so I could beat those two (in terms of academic grades. Not physically involved, alright.) Frankly speaking, all I was thinking were to improve myself instead of being competitive with other students. Competitive at times to improve, yes. But I'm not doing it to show that I can be better than those bullies. Wasting my time. Yet, explaining to people, even Dhia herself was technically pointless because I'm starting to doubt that people around me would understand what I was thinking at that time. Different perceptions as if something odd in here so not much of talking back since it drained my energy over unnecessary things. Surprisingly enough, that also happened while Tijah, Hanna, Dhia, and I played truth or dare. Never have I thought that being honest would have earned me an unexpected answer from Dhia. "So, Fida...what's the thing that you never told people about?" She asked. I chose Truth by the way.

"Okay...umm...I used to have my own imagination while my parents off to work. Y'know, like being a witch while sweeping the floor and stuff. Hehe." I admit that it was rather childish and embarrassing to me but a game is a game. Her response caught me off guard. Purely unexpected.

"You imagined those things while you're home alone?" She repeated the statement I've mention.

"Well, yeah?" I chuckled.

"Fida, you need help if that's the case. I'm afraid you've gone mad."

She said.

I've batting my eyes to hear such a shocking reply, "I'm sorry, what? Mad?" I had a thought she was probably pulling a prank so I simply laugh about it. She look serious about it and even tried to gain approval from the rest – Tijah and Hanna. They even look worried about that matter and suggested I go see a psychiatrist. Good lord, I never imagine a small difference in perceptions could be this far off. I tried to deny their thoughts of it with awkward laughs but they seemingly stick to it instead, convincing me to see the doctor. I shrug it off and simply say okay. Did I go to see a doctor? Nope. I'm honestly surprised that Dhia came from an urban place like me so I didn't see that coming. Oh, well. I just slide it off like some sort of lame joke, though.

The fact that Dhia and I were close like sisters, means that we technically went for laundry and bought lunch together. Dhia asked me to teach her how to wash clothes. By the time I tried to teach her, she suddenly said need to attend something and will be right back. Perhaps I've been too kind for my good that I eventually washed her clothes to the end along with mine, instead of letting her do her chores. Tijah saw this. She didn't seem very pleased. Hanna and Tijah also noticed the fact that Dhia went to lunch with me most of the time. She told me that she tried to save money, and feared the fact that she's been a burden to her family. Her parents struggled to find money to accommodate her two siblings who are still in school. I felt sorry for her and agreed to help her with that matter. Knowing that I have the desire to buy some other things as well made me rethink three to five times to survive with the available money that I've got because I had to share my money with her while buying lunch.

It was all until a big misunderstanding occurred between me and our two roommates, Suria and Rose. There was one time they locked me out of the room at night. After opening the door and going back to their own bunk, one of them chirped, "Oh, look! Someone just got back to her nest!" Then the three of them guffawed in loud laughter. I'd say that Dhia's true nature started to show more clearly than ever. Picking their side when it benefits her for some sort of 'protection'. We both no longer went to class together as we used to and it didn't bother me one bit. I've made new friends along the way. It felt much lighter when she was not around me. Neither did I feel sleepy when I sat solo in class instead of beside her. Though I did wonder how on earth I still felt sleepy in class whenever I sat beside her, even though I've made sure I've had a good hour of rest and sleep. Weird.

Hanging out with my new friends made me feel refreshed. I did get social anxiety sometimes but they seem genuinely open about it too. We played to make up among us girls in Arlina's room. Experimenting with shades of lipstick got me intrigued. And I never expect them to call me pretty. My mental find it shocking, though. Why, it felt like the first time I heard people outside of my family circle (besides my Mom, that is) call me gorgeous. I just giggled and thought they were just being polite. The girls insisted that I look damn different with red lipstick. I supposed I should say thank you but also felt shy about it. We took the picture as memoirs. One of the pictures of me wearing red lipstick suddenly been shown to my roommates. "She looks like a whore to me." Tijah casually commented, causing Dhia and Rose to burst into a laugh. I would consider it a big lie if I said I didn't feel any pain.

It's not like things like this ever happened before. There was one time before we had a huge fight, I wore a black and purple scarf with tiny chequered tiles along the sides while I was getting ready for class. Rose suddenly commented, "Hey, Fida, those scarf looks super ugly! Better change that before you've embarrassed yourself." It caught me speechless. My brain technically loading to hear such absurdity. "Yeah, that scarf is damn ugly! Why are you wearing them anyway?" Suria and Dhia nodded in agreement. I didn't assume they knew that the scarf was bought by my mother.

And I didn't suppose my logic would penetrate any blockheads either. "So which color am I supposed to wear?" Technically I demand a solution that they've made a stupid urgency for me to change in spite of giving off an awkward smile. "I don't know. Just change something else." Suria shrugged it off before shifting her attention back to her Blackberry. Figures. But I just remain silent and did my own thing. Of course, the jokes didn't stop there. "Damn someone being weird in this room I swear that person acting like retard or maybe Autism." As much as I find it exhausting to 'watch' those cheap dramas unfold, I didn't think I have many choices but to change it to typical soap drama instead. Too bad there's no remote to change the channel.

I wasn't sure how long it has been. Fatigued, but at the same time felt happy about it because I am literally free as a bird. No need to think much if anyone finds it rather an uncommon thing to do. And to my surprise, Dhia came up to me while they went out with their other friends. I didn't expect Dhia remain sitting in the room. Thinking she was probably off with those two to wherever they went. I love the quiet ambiance that is about to happen. "Hi." She greeted me with smiles, taking a seat next to me. "Hi," I replied while doing my own revision. Apparently, she came to apologize for not being able to stand up for me in the needed time and claimed that she too, became the duo's snarky jokes. "But you shouldn't blame them because you, too, made a big mistake." Somehow the last sentence caught me by surprise. Not trying to be egoistic, but I've sensed something off from her confession. Right, I did accidentally have my fair share of the mistake but I wonder why her intonation as if putting all the blame on me as the main root of such a mess. Though, I kept it silent. Not wanting to drag more stupid drama between me and her. I want my peace, please. Thank you.

"Ever since the four of us got into a fight, I didn't have friends to have lunch with." She added. "Those two often went out without me." I just hum and nodded to her every word. Not proposing a single solution to that. Soon, things went back to as they used to. Just as you would've guessed. I and Dhia became close once again. I actually had a hunch that if I were with her, again, I would have to share my money pockets during lunch. "Besides, our Moms are close so it wouldn't be good if both of us still fighting like this." She stressed her point rather casually. That's when the situation became hard to escape. My parent felt glad to know that I have a best friend. It's a good thing, they said. While having a best friend is a good thing to have in life, I couldn't shake the feeling that part of me felt heavy to be close with Dhia again. However, because of that reason, treating Dhia like a casual friend instead of a best friend became impossible. Wouldn't want to make my Mom feel troubled either. Hence, I followed the flow and enjoy my time at the university with Hanna, Tijah, and Dhia.

Of course, things weren't always as lovely as one would have hoped. I've found myself in another cold fight with Hanna, Tijah, and Dhia. I honestly had no idea how and why it happened. Misunderstanding again? I did catch glimpse of sheer annoyance once or thrice. I remembered that one time during English speaking practice with Madam Suzanna. The four of us agreed to come as one group. Everything went smooth yet the conversation flow was plainly dull. So I spruced up some silly questions. Our topic was based on the impact of social media on children along with its advantages in process of learning.

"Okay, so how does the children are going to learn martial arts if they can't attend proper classes?" I asked. Supposedly we end the session but I just happen to note that students will get extra marks if they raise an argument upon points. So I did that.

Madam Suzanna seems to smile at that, but not Dhia, nor even Tijah and Hanna. They glanced with frustration as I raised the question. Days after day befriended them as a group of four, my mind unconsciously thought that I may have caught myself in an awkward friendship where my presence was nothing but an addition to the number. Because I've noticed that only three of them look much closer. I've kept those thoughts buried, reminding myself that my perception betrayed me. I've tried to talk to them when the three of us are involved in a cold fight. But it felt absurdly awkward. The trio kept their distance away from me when I approached them. They told me I was being a self-centered and insensitive person. "Sorry..." I apologized. And they said apologizing wasn't enough to fix things. Hanna even added that friendship wasn't something that you could expect things in TV drama. Once again it caught me off guard. I wasn't sure how it ended up this way. I remembered I've printed out past year's questions for four of us so that we can all study together in the library yet none of them responded. Hung their head low as if they've seen a ghost. Not uttering a single word at that. Perhaps my hype annoyed them to the core. Regardless, it's fine. I'm okay with it. If that's the way it is. And unknowingly the conflict soon took a phase of resolution as our current faculty moved to Raub.

How shocking to know that I've been assigned to the same room as her. Or rather, she made a deal with me before we get to enter the new room. A friend of mine named Sheila asked me to be her roommate but it was too late. Plus, Dhia has been begging me to stay in one room with her because I'm the only one who knew how to assist her when her migraine hit her again. Indeed, I've been tending to her headache issues before. Not saying that I knew well how to assist patients with a severe headaches. I mean, surely other people would have the possibility to learn that as well right? C'mon, we've got Google search nowadays, haven't we?

"Please, Fida...It's not that I don't trust other people. I wouldn't be sure that others would understand my case as much as you."

"We've got Google, right?" I replied in half jest.

"Alaa...please lah be my roommate." She pleaded again.

Honestly, I'm running out of options of roommates to share with. During our stay in Raub, each room should only consist of two students. Pretty much like how we had roommates in Machang where it totals up to four people. But here in Raub, each house had four bedrooms. These four bedrooms were meant for two students each. Everyone else was paired up, except me and Dhia. Oh wait, there's someone else who would like to ask her to be their roommate. But Dhia hesitantly rejected, stating that she had a roommate of her own—me. She pleads again. Made a cute expression as she tried her best to make me agree to it. I sighed. "Fine, then." That answer made her jump in delight. With that, my relationship with Hanna and Tijah soon recovered. I find it confused yet unbothered to dig more about it. Getting myself deep into emotional drama would only lead me to nowhere.

I learn to teach myself on forgiving others. Mum advised me about it as well. It's not that she's being ignorant about it. Mum felt shocked as much as Dad to know where my money had been spent.

"I spent my allowance on Dhia while we're hanging out together because she didn't want to burden her family..." Dhia and I made a promise not to tell a soul about it. The girl too spent her allowance on her secret boyfriend. As the result, she couldn't have enough money for her own survival.

"For god sake, her parents still working and they're capable to fund her study!" Dad roared, slamming the bank statement harsh on the wooden table in the living room.
I knew that. And I'm only done that to help her since she seem helpless. Also, the fact that both our parent shared strong relationship had me in quite dilemma. "Dear..." Mum hugged me tight.

"I'm so sorry, Mum..." All the pain that I've been keeping inside me flowed like river as I burst down into tears. "Mum, I'm so sorry..."

For the first time, I saw Dad crying. I couldn't quite read his exact expression. It lies between forlornness, sympathy toward his child, and disappointment over the whole situation. Treachery. Who would've thought a child of a parent with whom they both had been close all this while, led their daughter to a painstaking dilemma? Dad went amok to learn the betrayal that Dhia had caused. Mum tried her best to calm Dad. The truth soon spilled when Dad checked my bank account just in case I still had enough money for my upcoming spending in Raub later on. The necessities such as food and books. Or probably buying other things that may come from the faculty and all. "We can't actually claim the amount from her...what would her parent say to that..." Even Mum hesitated. Sighed in dilemma to learn the shocking truth. Mum looked me right in the eyes. Empathy filled her heart to note her daughter fell into a toxic friendship with Dhia. "If anything happens again, be sure to tell us about it..." Tears flowed out of her eyes. "Mum and Dad always love you no matter what... Okay?" I nodded.

First half semester in Raub, everything was like normal fun. No drama. I even found my favorite places to unwind at the new campus. Library and the bakery shop. I swear their Red Velvet cookies taste good! Even the other bakery goods like a twisted bun, homemade lasagna, mushroom soup, and sausage bread were so soft. On top of that, our law lecturer kept me noted on fresh Takoyaki and Okonomiyaki. Food wasn't the only thing that made me happy in the new place. A new place in a new fresh year in a new semester gave me a new hope of emancipation. My freedom to move around. It's not that I never had a chance to move around while we were in Machang. The distance between the library and dorm felt far that sometimes I had to use Giling (a yellow van to transport within the campus in Machang) to move around. It would have depended on my mood to go to the library.

As for Dhia, well, she still kept up her old habit. Sharing allowance as we both bought lunch together. Same excuses she used while we were in Machang. I pretended like I'm used to it. Except for the fact that I tried avoiding buying her lunch using my money as often as she get to have like back in the days. If she gave hint to me that she want something, I would casually nod to her and tell her, "Sure. Go ahead and buy them." With my arm folded while waiting for her outside of the convenience store, simply nodding head if she wants something. She smiled. Browsing over other things that caught her attention. Not long after that, Dhia walked out of the store empty-handed.

"Eh? You're not buying that snack? I thought you want them." I find it quite strange that she didn't came out with the things she wanted to buy. Well, it's common that you have a second thought when stepping into any mart, and end up not buying anything because you don't feel like it. I did wonder my instinct felt something off when it happened like twice times ever since that occurred. Probably I'm just being paranoid.

Dhia gave a small pout while shaking her head, "Never mind lah... maybe next time..."
"Oh...Okay." With that, the two of us head over to class.

Meeting new people from another region like Dungun who had the same faculty background as us from the Machang region earned Dhia a new best friend. Me? I find it adequate to befriend anyone regardless of gender and background on a cordial level. But Vivy and Inara are my new close friends in Raub. We bonded during IR class when we had to form a group presentation. Vivy, Inara, and I clicked right away. Both of them are already best friends from Dungun. We met up in the library occasionally to discuss our assignment topic. I felt open and my heart was completely wrapped in a warm, fuzzy sense of happiness whenever I'm around them. Really hope that I could be part of them like close friends, but I am also slightly afraid if I messed up things like how it happened in Machang. Therefore, I kept our cordial bond at its good point.

"Vivy is good with remembering dates of the historic event. I wish I could have abilities like yours..." I said. Even Inara agreed with me. No joking. To be able to remember specific dates of the historical event are just rare. I even found myself confused at times to remember which dates would it be.

"Not gonna lie, I'm with Fida!" She chirped in.

"What!? Seriously you too?" She chuckled, "Nah, everyone got their own specialities. Just go with what you're good at."

Spending time with them has opened my eyes to get out of my sickening trauma. Made my neurons feel refreshed to meet and have friends that are truly open about the world as well as life as a whole without being unnecessarily snarky to one another. It's unfortunate to say that my new dream which I highly believed would lead me to my very own private living space with my new friends, was suddenly interrupted by none other than Dhia for unnecessary reasons. Honestly, I find her behavior became odder and odder as we all moved to Raub. Knowing that she made new friends that shared the same vibe as she would be a good opportunity for me to start afresh. Sadly, she's been bloody clingy like a demanding child.

Tini, the new friend Dhia has made besides from Hanna and Tijah on the first day we attend classes in Raub. She's the *kepochi* little girl with plump, rosy cheek who often finds any, and I mean like – EVERY chance to remarked me as a sore thumb for being ugly among them. "Gonna put a sticker on Fida's face because she's so damn ugly that it will ruin our precious photos if we let it be! Hurry and put them on." She plainly stated with her eyes casted in sheer criticism. That was unexpected. I'm not even surprised that none of them opposed it. Neither did I expect she came down with us after class for some random selfie near the vending machine. Ironically enough she boldly sneaked up to me to see why I was laughing while doing my homework. TWO TIMES in a row, and even Dhia got curious but Tini volunteered to sneak up to see what I was doing. Do these humans even know the term called private space? Just leave me enjoying my homework while being fangirling over Archer Emiya, for god sake. I truly despise sharing my private matter so I quickly change my screen whenever she rushed up to see my screen. It's bloody annoying but luckily it happened on that day only.

And then there's another girl from Kelantan named Ijah. Dhia told me she was a bullied victim by her group of friends and was helpless to escape from her circle. For once, I no longer found empathy resided within my heart at that moment. I supposed the girl probably shared similarities as I've experienced back in Machang. Alas, my heart grew cold. "I see..." That was all I responded to her. Dear Dhia, go ahead and be whatever savior you want to be but leave me out of this. "She's all alone in the room and even in class. I was thinking that we should befriend her." She suggested. "Go ahead," I answered her. And she did. The two of us occasionally invited her over after class for lunch and study group. Taking notes that these two fellows has become her new best buds, I assumed it should be best for me to have my own time to study and make some new friends without strings of attachment coming from her. So I hang out with Vivy and Inara for most of our study discussion sessions at the library. To my dismay, Dhia relentlessly called me. I ignored her. No time wasting. But the ringtone kept on distracting our discussion.

"I-I'm so sorry, guys." I apologized to Vivy and Irana for the abrupt inconvenience.

"Nah, it's okay...we're gonna take a break for a while. I'm gonna grab some drink. Hey, Fida. Do you want something?" Vivy and Irana excused themselves for a while to grab some drinks and snacks as we decided to take a small break. "Umm...thanks, but I'll be fine." I politely smiled at them before exasperatedly sighing at the calls and messages. Damn, she's such persistent. I honestly felt lazy to call her back, especially while I'm in the library. Hate to disrupt the quiet ambiance everyone had in the room, so I texted her.

"What's up? You called?"

In instant, I received a reply from her. "Yeah...I was wondering where were you since this morning."

"Library. Why?"

"What were you doing there?"

"Study. Group discussion. Do you need anything?" I just hope she was merely asking. What else people were doing when they came to the library besides from studying? And hey, why would Dhia effortlessly called me if she could just send a text messages just to know where I've been?

"When are you going back?"

"I don't know. Until discussion over. Why?" Seriously my energy drained entertaining these endless questions.

"I'm scared. I'm all alone. Can you come back now?"

I'm not sure if others find this as cutesy but I certainly would it as 'What the heck!?' moment.

"Can't promise. Need to settle some assignment." I told her. Stressing out that our group had a dateline to attend and this is the time we get to settle the work together as a group. The messages ended by the time Vivy and Irana came with some snacks and canned drinks. "Wait! We could eat and drink here?" I looked at them with sheer surprise. "Just don't bring *Nasi Lemak* or *Durian* in this room." Vivy casually jested. 24 Hour Room was just outside the library which was open from 6 a.m to 12 p.m for all students to cram their revisions. Not really clocked for 24 hours, but it was worth it if the students forgot to bring their matric cards yet wish to have a quiet time of revision. Ten minutes after that, my phone vibrated again. Signalling the incoming call from none other than Dhia, I heavily sighed and ignore it. "Hey, are you okay, Fida?" Vivy asked me. "Someone's been calling you. Probably it's important." Irana looked at me with concern. "It's okay. Just pick it up. Must be urgent." She added. Again, we paused our session just to allow me to pick up the call.

"Hello?"
"Fida, I'm scared...can you just come back now? I'm not used to being alone..."

I felt that Vivy and Irana overheard her voice. Then, the two of them decided to stop the session for today and will continue on another day once I ended the call. I am embarrassed to cause unnecessary trouble for them amid our discussion. Luckily, turned out they didn't seem to mind. "No worries, Fida...Our brain got jammed with these hectic facts." Irana cordially made jokes out of it. Even though they seem genuine, I still felt bad about it. Still, I just agreed to the idea of meeting on another day to finish up our tasks. Waving at them while I'm on my way, I took a slow walk to calm myself down. I've tried not to let my emotions get over me. By the time I arrived at my room, I noticed there's the slightest light leaked into our assigned room in between two pairs of the hanging curtain. Didn't she know how to open them?

"What's up?" I asked, rather unfazed with the stupid calls.

"There's a monster under my bed." She nervously chuckled.

Dear god, I am well aware that I shouldn't curse nor use bad words regardless of how fuming I'm currently feeling right now. So I just zipped my mouth and let out a soft chuckle. To be honest I've had my head call her an utter dimwit. "Oh," I responded. She laughed at how silly things have been. I didn't know where were all my strength to endure these petty matters, but I let out a chuckle. She had no idea it was rather a sarcastic laugh instead of a chortle over her silliness. My body and soul were blanketed in mental exhaustion. Originally I was planning to have a self-study in the library instead of the room for a change of study atmosphere. Moreover, while Dhia was still in the room, I didn't have the option to have some light for study because she said patients with migraine were super sensitive to light that it will make the headache ache even more. So, I silently walk out of the room for my self-study plan. This was truly unexpected when she called me just to accompany her because she got scared of the pitch-black room. She was nice at certain times, like ensuring I didn't wear pajamas down the dining hall because it was inappropriate.

At the same time, her logic was purely out of logic. Often she stated her beloved brother's into the narration to prove that she's being real. As much as I've trained myself to be independent ever since, in Machang, I did a similar pattern in Raub where I went back and forth with my routine. That includes walking solo to class because the waiting group of friends on our way to class felt like taking too much time for me to stand or sit there awkwardly. Not that I hate it. I didn't mind but I can be quite impatient for sake of waiting when I could just wait for them at the class instead. Same thing. Hanging out was done like normal. Just want to have some space from time to time. Oddly enough, a distinct pattern of behaviour in Dhia slowly drove me nuts sometimes. Not always she went nuts over small petty things. I usually tend to shrug it off after that. But once in a while, Dhia's nature of controlling freak became worse. There was one day that I felt lazy to wait for Dhia and her new friend to get ready for class. I didn't tell them but I figured they should have noticed. Besides, I'm in a rush. I figured they wouldn't mind either and being understanding. To my surprise, Dhia personally DM me via Whatsapp with a long manipulated, twisted preaching—reminded me to know my place. The message sounded like this (I seriously felt a rush of laziness to digest her whole point even if she provide it in bullet form...)

"Just so you know I had done numerous things for you including spending my allowance for your lunch and so on. You don't seem to appreciate a single thing I've done for you all these years and I've grown tired of your pathetic behavior. Know your place, Fida!

I'm the one been taking care of you all this while so be grateful! Stop being immature. You're already a grown-up so be ashamed of yourself."

...It was my allowance, to begin with, and Dhia didn't fulfill her promise to pay the amount as she said. All she ever gave were just excuses and more excuses. If I ever being particularly cumulative on every single cent she 'borrowed' from me, plus with ticket bus that I HAD to PAY (estimated three times yet the ticket cost RM 50 per head) on her behalf while we all decided to go home by bus from Machang—I might have made a thousand Ringgit for all the debt she owed me. My friend, Frida, is one of her victims too. She lend her RM 5 since she forgot to bring her wallet to buy lunch. Unlike me, Frida relentlessly demands Dhia to pay back her RM 5. Disappointed or not, Dhia paid her back the same amount. To that, I knew I should have done like how she did in the first place. I should be more strict. "Being nice is good. But you have to be careful, otherwise, she'll turn you into her slave for benefits." Frida advised me.

Speaking of slavery, I happened to have a suspicion about Dhia when one of her friends named Ema came to our room with some financial emergency. Technically, no one knew my background. Except for Dhia. I didn't suppose anyone here knew my parent's car or how much allowance I'd spent for a week. I assumed everyone was on an equal level, including me. Either way, I kept my mouth shut when it comes to financial matters because it was sensitive to privacy in the most logical sense. There were like 5 people in the room, including Dhia and me, and Ema consistently edging me to help her out. Promised to pay me back on after that. I've run out of excuses to reject her offer. Even Dhia edged me to help the poor girl. Groaned. I went to help her that night. Luckily the ATM machine was available nearby, but I was hoping the machine was out of service at that time to save me. Too bad. The machine works out well. Ema instantly made a transfer to my account, right in front of my eyes. She paid the exact same amount. "Hey, Fida...thank you. If you weren't here, my brother would be in big trouble." She thanked me. "Yeah, sure. You're welcome." I plainly answered, and we both went back to our room.

I realized that I might have found myself late in being strict. I supposed parent relations were meant to remain at that, and to that borders only. In other words, it shouldn't be a major effect in a way of affecting me to assist her most of my time even when things didn't need to be attended to (like things that she can just do on her own). Albeit, I'm still determined to not take orders from her in any way possible. Partially regretful for having a soft-hearted nature, because guilt-trip game made it easy for me to feel sympathy for people. Unconsciously inviting danger into my life than avoiding them. If this was a fictional or manga character that I've accidentally found in my collection, I would have facepalmed, yet here I am, similarly to that fictional character who was entrapped in a twisted mind game of a girl who claimed to be my best friend. Thinking back these sickening memories made me wonder how on earth have I made it this far. Surviving an emotional game wasn't as easy as pie. Her twisted nature became obvious week by week. Even during her mother's visit to our room, she managed a sweet, innocent smile while claiming that she's been taking care of me all years of studying together.

"I've been taking care of her ever since the beginning." She smiled. I instantly despise to hear those faux claim coming from her mouth.

"No! Actually I'm the one—" I quickly interjected, but she's not giving up either. So Dhia quickly jumped into the debate of 'Who taking care of Who' throughout study years.

"Alright....Alright....That's enough. It doesn't matter whose taking care of who, as long as both of you made it safe and peace throughout the study." The middle aged woman settled down the argument by turning the situation into neutral.

If only her mother knew the real situation, I wonder what would she think?

Each semester, students had to register for their room as well as their roommates. To be perfectly honest, I've made lots of Dua to save me from this misery and I truly hoped that Dhia had been approached by someone else as her new roommate. It was probably some sort of mother's instinct. After I helped Dhia carry her stuff up to her room, her mother gently came up to me and gave some food for Dhia and me. As if she held high hope that I was still Dhia's roommate.

"How was study?" She asked.

"Study was fine. Hehe." I replied as polite as possible with unfaltering smile.

"Fida...you seem to try avoiding Dhia...Are you two okay?" She asked. To be clear, that was right on the spot. Just like how I'd prayed to be separated from Dhia after all things that happened because I've grown fatigued with those sick mind games. Seriously, I demand my personal peaceful space.

"Eh, no *lah*. Everything's fine, auntie. It's just that I've been very busy with study. I didn't want to disturb her either because sometimes she had severe migraine and I feel bad to turn on the lights." Part of it was both truth, and lie. I did study outside of the room because the scenario literally urged me to be considered with her illness. Lies—It was also means to avoid Dhia and everything was not fine as she had imagine. Come to think of it, after coming back from event, I had to make a report as quickly as possible because I wouldn't want the ideas to just flowed away. In my defence, I was thinking that I've done a fair share to lower down the brightness of my laptop while doing my work in the pitch black room (because of her migraine...) where Dhia's limb was facing the white wall instead of my direction. There, I supposed the bright shouldn't bother her. I was mistaken.

"Fida...what are you doing?" She asked me in rather sleepy state.

"Umm...I'm need to do some work. Some report. Why?"

"Oh, no...just asking, because the lights feel too strong."

"...I've lowered down the brightness." Sighed. I lowered more the brightness of my computer. "Better?"

"Still there's some lights..." Noting the answer, I started to have a doubt that she meant 'zero light, please...my migraine can't handle them...'

Not that I've been trying to be protesting much, although I've tried (like leaving her behind when walking to class. EVERY class), I was thinking that night was an exceptionally tiring day for me yet I'm in full spirit to spruce up my writing ideas for the report with hope it charmed my lecturer to give me extra marks. And this kind of predicament happened. Sucks. The other girls were having dinner outside of the room, I didn't want to bother them with homework pressure I may accidentally cause. And by the meaning of extremely tired, I mean I'm utterly fatigued to even walk to the library at night.

"Don't mind me...just cover your face with pillow or whatever." I calmly negotiated while suggesting her to use other type of means to help herself sleeping in a dark room.

"Hope you'll be able to settle your work fast because the lights making my head hurt..." And then she turned her body facing the white wall again, forcing herself to sleep. I just hum in response and continue my work. Barely made it in a full draft, but I'm still not feeling satisfied because it felt that I need to double check my writing points in case I've missed something while writing the report. Due to the fact Dhia previously insisted me to turn off the lights, I decided to close my laptop and continue on the next hour when she wake up. Luckily I've able been given chance to send the report on two days after the event. Knowing that everyone were completely washed out with the one full day programme.

My friendship with Dhia was one heck of a roller coaster. I would like to think that it was normal to everyone. Argument between friends, especially when your friendship getting closer and longer over the years. I mean like getting used to other person's behaviour, different pattern of thinking, perceptions and perspectives, as well as family background. I couldn't care about family background. I literally treated everyone same. Even as much as Dhia told us how her family blood line connected to some prestigious connection, I've technically treated her no different from my other friends. If you're good, then you're okay in my book. If not, It's not even worth my attention to learn more about you and do acknowledge that you're very much welcome to get out from my life. Pretty much I've made it obvious. Even when she asked me to do the translation because she's not used to English. It's a complicated language for her yet she refuse to take effort for it either. Just to be clear, I never considered my English on an excellent level as she or some of my friends would have claimed. I was always thought my English was around passable grade instead of proficient level. Besides, I still have long way to learn and it's a continuous journey.

To my dismay, she forced me to do it in spite of chuckling over it as if it was funny. I made a firm decision to pause. One assignment down, and the other one can be done after taking shower. "Nope! Sit here and do the work." Her hand strongly pulled me down, back to my seat. "I need to take shower. Not feeling comfortable right now..." Somehow I'm feeling drenched in sweat after coming back from class with Dhia. The weather was a bit hot that day, too. Plus, my hands were shaking in fatigue, too. I had my hand writing lots of thing in one day and then I had to cram over the assignment even though we're using Microsoft Word.

All she did was gave a vague idea for the points. Refused to switch places with me for 5 minutes of testing out herself to take my place for writing out the points. Damn, her biggest point her was literally simply ordering people around without actually engulfed into work nature of it. While we're getting half part of the assignment essay up to notch, Dhia opened her mouth as she expressed her hope to be my roommate in the future semester. "We've got few more semesters to go, Fida. Let's try our very best!" Oh, when I said she expressed her hope, it was much more like her demand on getting into it rather mere hope. "Nah, I'm changing roommates next sem." I plainly stated while typing. Boy, I am fully aware she's one hot-tempered damsel, but I never would have guessed she would went far by pulling my scalp, deeply, while threatening me, "You won't get a chance to be other people's roommate!" Dhia then casually laughing as she ordered me to continue the work. Lucky my head didn't bleed, but I was sure enough starting to despise physical contact from human being after what she just did. Filth. And I meant that by what she had done. It disgusted me deeply.

Apart from revising subject syllabus, I did myself some side reading on Best-Friend topic—How to know if you were a best friend to someone, a normal friend, or just a friend with benefit. Dhia and I were literally close. Went to class and lunch together. That leaves the choice between Best Friend and Friends With Benefit Category. Dhia's behaviour was like between these two category. Unclear, grey area at that. While she demanded a lot of things, ordering me around here and there, Dhia can be rather concern at times. She helped me with study hack and maths. Even so, they're not as much as when she needed something out of me in the crucial times. The stupid request at that. My instinct believed that it was nearly impossible to considered our friendship in a genuine Best Friend bond after weeks contemplating her pattern of behaviour as well as consequences I received whenever I acted against her expectation. Such simple thing as emitting lights from the devices. Even her friends siding with her, including that mak cik kepochi. Nevertheless, I constantly continued my study routine as usual. Had a break time and study again. I didn't want to hate her either because that's just sapping my energy over silly stuff. Mum felt sympathy but neither did she could do more about it either, so she advised me to just being nice but careful at the same time. Also, just focus on study.

Talking about study, Dhia had borrowed my printed past year papers as I was doing my revision since she decided to help the girl named Ijah. At first it was fine. I mean I literally let it slide. She's probably forgot. But by the time I need to use it, she hasn't return it to me. Thought she said sekejap which referred as momentarily (?). She did invited me to join along. I tried. And I was being ignored. Except for Ijah. What went frustrating was when she asked me to wait for her as we head over for lunch time. Guess what? I've waited for AN HOUR to the point I felt asleep waiting her to get ready, turned out she already went out with Ijah to buy lunch.

"Eh, Fida...so sorry...I forgot to inform you that Ijah invited me for lunch on ad hoc..."

So ad hoc occurrence made people unable to send message? Not once, but twice. Second time was when she asked me to accompany her to somewhere nearby. So we made a deal to waited downstairs at the usual spot near the laundry machines which meant for the students of the assigned block. Guess again, dearies. An hour of waiting earned me another walk to the spot near library because she's already went there. Obviously contradict from the information I had from her on earlier. The group discussion ended and Dhia proposed to go somewhere outside the campus on lunch with Ijah. I found myself snickered, laughing sarcastically upon the abrupt changes. "Now that we've done discussion. Gotta go." I excused myself and went to attend whatever need to be done. Have I ever cried over these sort of betrayal? Not anymore. I just wonder why bother to drag me to this extent? To kill some time? For god sake, find other people as a victim, will you, Dhia?

Upon Dhia's 'ad hoc' lunch event outside of Raub campus, Hanna and Tijah came into my room. I greeted them with usual hi, and the two of them seems cautiously stepped into my room as their eyes glanced left and right side of the room. "What's up?" I mouthed. "Is she's here?" Tijah asked. "Dhia." She clarified. "We're thinking to meet you downstairs." Hanna gave an assuring smiles. I told them that she went outside for lunch, hanging out with several other friends. They nodded. Asked me if I was busy at the moment because they wish to discuss something with me this instance. I didn't expect anything. Besides, I was taking some break time before continuing my revision. Part of me felt that these two can be trusted despite the misunderstanding we had back in the days. It was purely misunderstanding that neither of us see it coming. To my surprise, there were other of my friends that I've known yet happened to had sleepover at their room during our stay in Machang which occurred while I involved into huge cold fight with Suria, Rose and Dhia. "Fida," One of them greeted me with warm smile.

"So...did you know why we're all being here?" Arlina calmly spoke.

"Uh...no?"

"It's actually because of you."

"Me?" Okay, that seriously got me confused.

"Yeah." Tijad stated. "The reason we fought with Dhia, was because of you." Oh my, that made me confused even more. Was that a bad thing or good thing?

"Sorry..." I apologized in advance.
"Don't be. It's because...we're trying to protect you actually. That's why we no longer walk alongside with Dhia starting from those days." Yeah, I still remember how Hanna and Tijah was close to Dhia but eventually went separate ways after few days later.

“We’ve watched everything she had done to you. Asking you to sleep on the floor to protect her from the monster under her bed —That’s downright low! She’s bullying you, Fida!” Tijah’s calm composure shook in latent rage as she spoke about Dhia.

“Last time we had discussion with her. She said something like “Fida is such a spoiled brat. As if she’s the only one who has a mother coming here!” And then she said, “I’m gonna teach her some lesson.” I was thinking that Dhia was referring the time my Mum came up to our room and I hugged her like a 5 years old child. My parent are the only precious treasure I have in life. I didn’t have siblings like Dhia. I supposed she have her mother too who always came up visiting her on Weekend. Ironic. By the term lesson in that context, I’ve clearly understood that she meant to bully me.

“She even asked you to buy her lunch—Like ALL THE TIME!” One by one, the girls expressed their frustration over Dhia’s behaviour. I have no idea how and why, this sort of meeting and solidarity alike, coming from them made me cry. But I refused to let my guard down so I hide them with a sheepish chuckles. To be honest, I’ve almost lost will and energy to laugh about it any longer yet I’ve been too tired to made it as main highlight of attention either. “Thank you…” was all I could uttered to them.

Sometime after that day, though it might not obvious, Dhia as if grown suspicious of me. If I ever to walk up personally to other classmates to ask something instead of her, Dhia too came up next to me while I was discussing with the students regarding the questions the I didn’t understand. I felt like I’ve been depending on her before so I decided to change perspective and asked other person instead. Regardless she thought me behaving suspiciously, I kept on my new behaviour to study. That also include sitting next to other classmates instead of next to her. And when she asked if I was okay, I just answered that I’m fine and went on with my routine— revision, assignment, watching anime, meal time, and hanging out with friends like normal. Even by the time Dhia went home on weekend, my wave to her was short and simple even with a smile. I didn't wait long for her silhouette to disappear from the stairs.

Another cold fight apparently occurred after Dhia threw my white pen drive as she helped fixing the format that suddenly went disarray. Probably because everyone was feeling exhausted so it kind of made sense I felt irritated to know she threw my pen drive to me while she's still mad for taking over my responsibilities in arranging everyone's part under one document while maintain the paper format that about to be printed out before we could submit to the lecturer. As I went back to my room, I tried to take as much time as I could to calm my nerves and think carefully—of my wrong doing and how to fix this. I'm still mad over her attitude in giving my pen drive in rather rude manner, but then again it could be both parties were at fault as well. Facing face to face with people can be such hassle. I had experience with Dhia, Tijah and Hanna while we had conflict in Machang. It didn't work well although Dhia literally provoked me to deal things face to face rather than messaging. And yes, when I tried to message her (just in case she still in bad mood if I straight came up to her to ask about the thing earlier which I wouldn't want to make things worst), Dhia coldly asked me to ask Suria. Sigh. I messaged Suria if I need to pay for the new printing they had after the new editing. None. The silent treatment went longer than I expected.

Not only that, her former gang which she had in Machang (all Machang students were transported to Raub campus) even seems to make a plan to lock the door as everyone else was already inside there, attending the lecture. I'm done with these typical asinine fools they had me in. Studying made it harsh with this sort of stupidity. Yet they look to enjoy it. I kept on studying, studying, and studying. Because that's my main sole purpose coming here. To learn. And even if death befalls them, I couldn't care less. Been called ugly more than once even by Dhia herself? Checked. Been disturbed by Dhia during the lesson by Sir Anuar and Sir Khairul on law and international relations? Checked. I've been patiently waiting to toss her away out from my life. Until I am no longer able to recollect my sanity with her absurdity. I've kept her locked outside the room, just like how she did to me before when she said the door never locked and yet it never budged no matter how many times I've tried, along with other roommates from another room. "OPEN UP THIS DAMN DOOR!!" She yelled. Banging the door hard as possible to threaten me to open them. My tears were all dried. My empathy went dead. I let her go insane outside of the room, unlocking the door. Until her mother came to her assistance.

My mum told me as well that Dhia's mother complained about my attitude towards her daughter. Although mum gave her a vague answer, she believed that I won't create such a fuss unless something happened to her. "She should have to check her daughter instead…hmph." Mum expressed her frustration over the situation. It's only a few weeks left until the final and the whole Diploma life will be over. The resolution soon literally resolved over the group chats— Me, Dhia, and some of our roommates. Despite coming to a neutral conclusion, Dhia remains cynical about me. "I'm surprised someone as you came from Madrasah school yet didn't behave like one." The text gave a clear sneer at me. Well, I was about to retort back to claim that she came from a top prestigious school in Malaysia and had high grades throughout our Diploma years of study yet still numbskull. Here's the thing. School background got nothing to do with people's behavior representation. Human background can be influenced by a lot of factors. Teaching me some lesson to be tough my arse!

The day of breaking free of the hellish nightmare came to light. My parent's bond with Dhia's parents was affected. It's not a good thing on the most logical basis if you ever ask any elders or youngsters. Cutting out human bonds wasn't a good thing in any religion either. However, there were times when such unpredictable events happen, some other things may have to be sacrificed. In my case, severing my bond means severe the parental relation both our parents had regardless of how strong one may claim it be. I've avoided as much as I can until the whole situation edged me to turn the table. She's not the only one who has emotions. The other had it, too. I am no exception to feeling mad about this bloody mess of a hellish drama that drained my mental energy to the core. Here's the thing that I hate to spell out —I was afraid of the sin of severing the bond between humans. Then Dhia flipped the card of guilt by pointing out our parent's close friendship made me feel guilty even more. Those things were all in Machang. Studying in Raub with fresh new air and new ambiance, brought me a new hope of changes—For sake of myself. That's when the changes of my attitude toward her. Towards the whole situation. Incrementally broke the boundaries that I've feared the most. As I search more for the sin of breaking bonds with humans we've met, there were exceptions to that matter. Meaning, that I didn't need to force myself to invest in such toxic friendship if brought harm more than good.

Thank goodness to Him for giving me strength to study and earned myself good grades. It's not full flat as my parent would have hoped, but they still feel grateful for it. My parent and I had a small celebration to it. I had myself successfully graduated from my Diploma.

And now the sickening dilemma has come to an end, still, the trauma of toxic friendship took me time to get rid of it. Neither did those bullies nor Dhia properly apologized for the things they had done. Neither did we ever meet again after that. It was all for good. I managed to proceed to the Degree level. Turned out we met again. But we're no longer in the same faculty. Same campus but different faculty. She started exchanging greets as we bump into one another. I just greet her out of courtesy. That's that. Occasionally Dhia asked me to accompany her since she's all alone. I honestly didn't know what I felt but it was nothing as close to sympathy. Just to kill some time? Probably. My friend who also made it to Degree, the same campus as me but same faculty as Dhia, advised, "Be careful, Fida...Don't let her trample you again..." She said. I took her advice in mind. Whether she went to influence people or so, I had no interest nor control over it either. So I lived up my life to the fullest. My principle remains the same: For sake of myself instead of others. This turned out to pay me back the money she owed me as we went to the mall by Grab that day. Just not the money I paid for her lunch all these past years. I don't suppose she spill the whole truth to her parent regarding the root of that mess either—Just to ensure some reputation she holds pride along her life as a respected individual perhaps. While we were walking at the mall, Dhia and I had a random conversation. I teasingly gave an idea about a girl who been bullied but only to found out that she's been backstabbed all along'. "That sounds familiar..." She looked as if awkwardly smiling. Of course, I quickly covered it off, "Nah, probably coincidence..." Well, whatever. We're no longer close as before. Just cordially neutral good terms. Dhia said she kept our hang-out meeting a secret because her parent became disapproved of my friendship with her ever since that conflict ignited.

Toxic trauma is like remnants of a plague. It's still there even if we've lived past the year of such an event. Faded? Indeed, they eventually became as thin as Samosa skin. But they're not completely disappeared. Mum once advised me that Fate chose me to walk that path for some reason. Perhaps a change of something. Perhaps an opportunity to be closer to Him by elevating our Ibadah. Our prayers. If it didn't change Dhia, then it was meant to change me. You might think Dhia was right all along and I was exaggerating things. It's okay, I leave personal opinions to you. All I ever wanted to share here is to value yourself more than your best friend(s). I do understand that it can be frustrating, but not every single thing is meant to be sacrificed for friendship. Learn to love yourself more. Much more than you love your best friend, because who knows they could replace you at any second if they find you unbefitting to their advantageous prospect. Now that I rethink about it, maybe there's no need to be so savage to show how strong you are. Be firm with your principle. And reasonable about it, too.

Frankly speaking, I feel like there is more to it that I wish to share with you. But I don't suppose I could remember it at this moment either. You see, life is full of wonder and may go beyond one's misery if we look at a different perspective. It's almost like two sides of the same coin, isn't it? While I've found myself obliged to take care of Dhia, I supposed not every part of her is that bad on a scale of 100 percent (probably just a balance of 50%...and the other 50% is...kindness?). She did teach me things or two. In her way, that is. And I still have my rights to reject her ideas of living in such a manner as she may similarly share with her other friends who uphold the same principle as her. I know now that egoism needs no further approach to debate. Best to ignore. I eventually learned this as Dhia and I once debated over McDonald's products. She loved them so much that she stood firmly upon that stance while urging me to join the crowd. I, myself, am not much into McDonald's (sorry to burst your bubble. Not hating it. Just not my thing...there's a difference to it that most people failed to understand). I gave her my point of view when Jamie Oliver exposed McD's hidden secret on their product quality on media. It triggered her and claimed McD is the top healthiest food in the world compared to other products. To ensure that no further silly debates went on from her, I just nod and agree with her points (... though I'm not. I still prefer other brands like KFC, Burger King, and Ramly Burger which I found prices are reasonable for the product they give to the customers. Note: theirs are much meatier than McD...sorry about that. This is just my personal opinion. Go ahead and have your McD). And it kind of works. And just so you know, egoism has nothing to do with gender. Females can be egoistic and stubborn as much as male.

Last but not least is to appreciate all the things people done to you, even in the slightest bit. Some people find it hard, under certain circumstances. It's understandable. In case you find yourselves in shoes of Dhia, I hope that you could stop taking advantages of your close friends to your benefits. Of course, you do enjoy having free benefits that you extracted from your dear friends—money, popularity, etc. But you never know the consequences of your doing in the near future. It doesn't happen now in this life, you might get it in the Afterlife where the punishment are much more...severe. Stop being manipulative and learn to appreciate your friends regardless how imperfect they may be. Even the perfect human named Muhammad S.A.W never took granted of every people he met along the journey. He welcomed them with warmth greetings. And if the person ever infuriate him to any extent, he leave those matters to Allah S.W.T and keep on spreading kindness to everyone, including non-Muslim.

As for someone like me, I hate to break it to you but do keep in mind that expecting nice things in return of our kindness are actually can be a massive scam. "Do good and people will do good to you," they say. I'm so sorry but that rarely happened to me. Though, people whom outside from my close circles—I mean other than someone like Dhia, Suria and Rose—They have been real nice to me. I wasn't sure if it's out of sympathy, but I do realize that they're good people with genuine good heart. Perhaps, on that point, we might as well rephrase that quote to something like this: We do kindness to people for sake of God. For sake of Allah. Yes, it is deeply painful to go through such path. But never cease to believe that God created a bright future for us someday if we ever keep on doing kindness. Life isn't always about materialistic. The fact that I managed to get good grades in spite of been mentally tortured by manipulative people might be part of His reward for the patience I had. It could be part of His tests. When God tests you, it's the act of showing His love to you—a sign that He missed your prayer. So please, never give up hope. Your family loves you. Your cats love you— they sure need you to bring snacks after all. Please believe that your life are worth more than you have right now. Just a little more patience, hope and changes of tactics to reach for the stars.

> *— I believe that you are more than what you know you're capable of. It's there. Deep within you.*

VOCABULARY

kepochi - The act of minding other people's business. Some local may call it as busybody.

Lah - A common slang used by local Malaysian.

Nasi Lemak - A type of local food where the rice is usually cooked with coconut milk, served with several slices of cucumbers, fried peanuts and anchovies, as well as Sambal and commonly boiled egg.

mak cik kepochi - Another word for mak cik bawang where it is often referred to someone who loves to poke their nose to someone else's matters.

Ohayogozaimasu - A Japanese term of 'Good Morning'. The simple of it is *Ohayo.*

Nasi Dagang - consisting of rice steamed in coconut milk, fish curry and extra ingredients such as pickled cucumber and carrots.

Nasi Kerabu - a Malaysian cuisine rice dish, a type of nasi ulam, in which blue-colored rice is eaten with dried fish or fried chicken, crackers, pickles and other salads. The blue color of the rice comes from the petals of Clitoria ternatea flowers, which are used as a natural food coloring in cooking it

Nasi Kukus - Steamed white rice with slices of cucumber , deep fried chicken and some *sambal.*

Takoyaki - a ball-shaped Japanese snack made of a wheat flour-based batter and cooked in a special molded pan. It is typically filled with minced or diced octopus, tempura scraps, pickled ginger, and green onion

Okonomiyaki - Okonomiyaki is a Japanese savory pancake dish consisting of wheat flour batter and other ingredients cooked on a teppan. Common additions include cabbage, meat, and seafood, and toppings include okonomiyaki sauce, aonori, katsuobushi, Japanese mayonnaise, and pickled ginger

Durian - Known as king of fruit. Have strong pungent smell despite of its soft, sweet taste.

Tomyam - Tom yum or tom yam is a type of hot and sour Thai soup, usually cooked with shrimp. Tom yum has its origin in Thailand. The words "tom yam" are derived from two Thai words. Tom refers to the boiling process, while yam means 'mixed'

ABOUT THE AUTHOR

Hikari Syuu

Preferably known as Hikari Syuu. A Malaysian author and student of UiTM. Writing has always been my dream ever since I was a kid. Luscious Bane is the very first piece that the author have started to introduce to the world where it was inspired by a real-life experience of a local student from one of the local universities in Malaysia who happened to experience a toxic friendship. "Luscious" technically referred as something sweet and innocent, which it literally been used as a term to described how friendship between Dhia and Fida was almost look harmless yet normal in the eyes of society, including from the perspectives of their respective parents at the early years of their bond. "Bane" is the second word that the author used as to indicates that their relationship as toxic, specially harmless to Fida. Though, the author would like to have her real name, as well as the real details of the event in this short story, remain hidden to avoid further defamation over the concerning individuals while maintaining the vital messages as a life lesson for the readers.

www.ingramcontent.com/pod-product-compliance
Lightning Source LLC
LaVergne TN
LVHW052106160826
845678LV00015B/3392

* 9 7 8 6 2 9 9 7 1 2 9 0 9 *